MEN IN THE SUN

BY DAVID LEDDICK

DESIGNED BY JASON LOSSER

UNIVERSE

For my great pal Benjamin Morrison, who brings so much sunshine to so many.

Excerpts from the following books are reprinted with permission from the publishers: Scary Kisses by Brad Gooch, published by G. P. Putnam's Sons, New York, 1988; With Duncan Grant in Turkey by Paul Roche, published by Honeyglen Publishers, London, 1982; The Sex Squad by David Leddick, published by St. Martin's Press, New York, 1998; Young Man from the Provinces by Alan Helms, published by Faber & Faber Inc., Boston and London, 1995.

First published in the United States of America in 1999 by UNIVERSE PUBLISHING, A Division of Rizzoli International Publications, Inc.
300 Park Avenue South • New York, NY 10010 • © 1999 Universe Publishing
01 02 / 10 9 8 7 6 5 4 3 2 • Printed in Singapore • Library of Congress Catalog Card Number: 98–61894
By David Leddick • Designed by Jason Losser

They are legendary, men in the sun. Icards, who flew too close to the sun, left his mark on mythology. When the wax that held his feathers in place melted, his beautiful body plunged into the sea in the full blaze of the sun. What was he looking for here, so near to the sun?

¶Phaeton, too, driving the chariot of the sun through the heavens, was painted on many ceilings that looked down on the Courts of the Louis in France. Always depicted as young and handsome and bold of profile and body.

¶My first memory of a man in the sun was a handsome sailor washing sails. I must have been about four years old.

Dianora Niccolini

¶In the small coastal town in Michigan where I lived as a child, a wealthy man kept his yacht moored. Al Pack was his name. A name that could only have belonged to a Prohibition rum runner. A Hemingway name for a Hemingway man. I saw him once. Short and smoking a cigar with a captain's cap on one side of his head. He

had a blond mistress, too. Did men like this exist before they wrote about them?

¶After Prohibition Al Pack found himself and his money in the depths of the Depression on the shore of our small lake, which fed into Lake Michigan. There he sheltered himself, his mistress, and his large sailing yacht. And from there he would sortie out in good weather into the "Big Lake," as we called it.

¶How sails get dirty I don't know. But the sails of Al Pack's yacht were being washed on a summer morning on our nearby school's tennis courts.

¶School was closed and my morning routine was to ride up the school hill on my tricycle to prepare myself for the event of going to kindergarten in the fall. This morning I saw a tall young man, stripped to the waist, hosing down the great spreads of canvas that covered the courts. He held a fire hose that was attached to a public fire hydrant. Al Pack knew the right people in our little town.

¶It was the first time I had ever seen anyone with

I really deep tan and their hair blonded from the sun. The young man must have been a sailor on Al Pack's yacht. Perhaps the youngest, who had been given the heavy work of scrubbing and hauling wet canvas about.

¶I was dazzled. Those shoulders, the tan, the naked upper body. I couldn't tell, really, if he was handsome. He was too much of a God for that.

¶I rode my tricycle to the side of the tennis courts and watched, transfixed. Maybe he was glad of the company, small as it was. He tried to talk to me. He smiled, laughed, called out questions. I said nothing. If Apollo had talked to you, would you have talked back?

¶I was waiting for something to happen, there in the sun, with the bronzed young man in the white sailor pants, slung low on his hips, rolled up on the bottom. What could have happened? I think I wanted him to take me away with him into the sunburned world he came from. A world where men were tall and blond and tan, standing on the

Dianora Niccolini

decks of their ships sailing into the sun.

¶No other child or adult appeared while I was there. I must have left him there eventually. My memory stops. But I certainly rode my tricycle back down the gently sloping hill, past Mrs Chisholm's heap of Victorian wooden lace and porches, all painted white. And pondered about being one with the Gods.

¶Isn't that what men in the sun conjure up for us? Not Christian gods. But pagan gods. Apollo, Hermes, Zeus, should we add Hercules? Long thighs strong chests, handsome fee and hands, squared- off chins and strong brows glowing and gleaming with the sun's bronzing.

¶Seeing this perfection, we want to possess it But can we ever? These are only harbingers o another world we hope exists . . . we dream exists . . . insist must exist. A world of beauty to be pursued all of our lives. This is a world tha exists for us, however briefly, as we regard men in the sun.

MEN COOLING OFF

BAIANO

1

Actually,

...the sun and I are almost

absolute strangers.

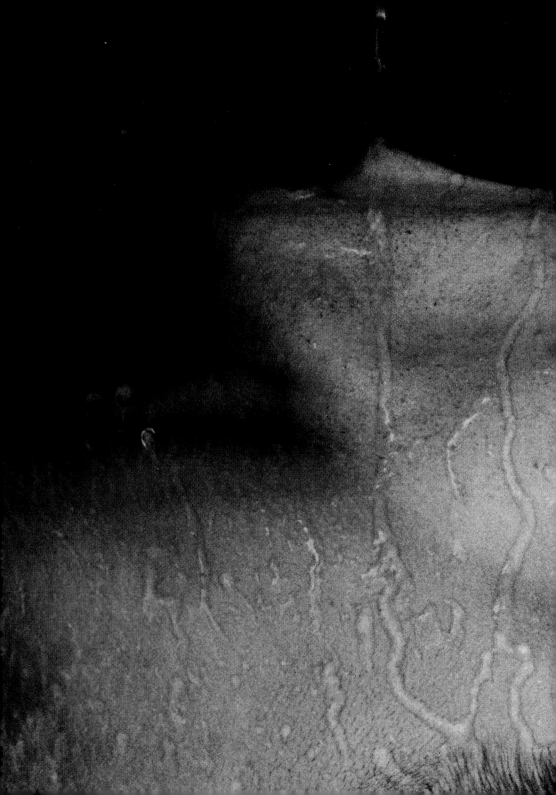

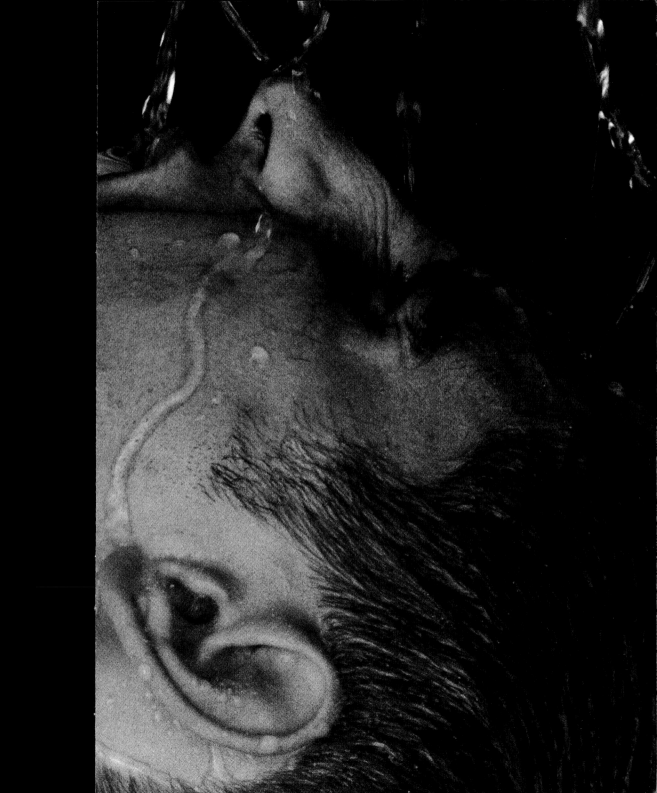

Since for much of  my adult life I was

paid to take off my clothes in front of

strangers as a model in an art

school, I could see little point in doing

so on a beach. And of course,

English beaches are not the exotic

tropical beaches

of Florida.

They are rainy and

windswept

tretches of pebbles

for the most

part. You are more

likely to get

goose bumps than

a tan on the

beaches of my

homeland.

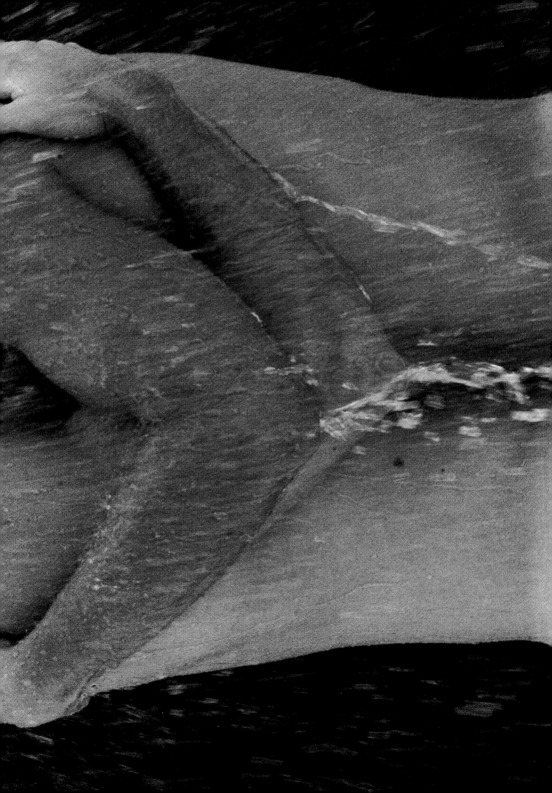

¶My one experience involving men who had obviously spent much time in the sun was in Boston, of all places. I had been invited to Boston one year to judge a bodybuilding contest. It was not very exciting. The contestants were pale and drawn. Enthusiasm was low. There was little to choose between one wan body and another.

¶But when I returned the following year all that had changed. Now the contestants were glowing with deep tans. Their oiled muscles rippled beneath the blazing lights. Music played. There were even potted palms on the stage. I was stunned and impressed.

¶I said to the manager of the contest that this was a great change from the previous year, as his large, blond, tan contestants swaggered about. And I added that it must, of course, be much more expensive. This took him aback. He stared at me, surprised at such a statement, and said, "Oh, but we shave each other." **—Quentin Crisp**

MEN UNDER THE SUN

2

NICCOLINI

¶ Clumsily, Todd gets up. The leftover smoke from last night's cigarettes stuffed in his throat like cotton. His cabin room is dark and anonymous and breezy. Sun registers on the pulled-down orange shade (litmus paper). He rolls apart from the sheets, one hairy leg hanging off the double-thickness mattress onto the floor, the other leg scissored up, one palm on scratchy chest, the other cupping matted sac of balls.

¶He sleepwalks through a shuffle on the floor of loose glossy magazine pages and rough newspaper sheets into the main room of the cabin. Pulls on some white chinos. He stands there. Twenty-four. Six feet. Brown wavy hair stuck in place from salt water. Skin dark from lying on the beach all week by himself. Cats eyes: transparent splotches of green, brown, blue, red, gray. Makes a half-smile to no one.

¶(It's not true that older men and women are any more likely to have spirits waking them up, or following them, than teenagers and young people. Twenty-four is a magic age.)

¶Todd makes a path through bullrushlike reeds, pinprick spears of grass. Over tracks brushed in the sand the night before by migrating snakes. The whites of his toenails and fingernails look ivory in contrast.

¶No one is around on Skunk Hollow Beach, an illegal beach on lower Long Island with condemned shanty shacks, condemned so the area can be turned into a state park. In the meantime a few squatters take advantage.

¶ Todd stretches in front of the in-full-blast ocean. The noisy birds in the stinkwood trees around the cabin can't be heard. He touches his toes. Bends from side to side. Then unzips his zipper and wriggles out of his white parchment pants. Lies down using his discarded pants as a beach blanket, but an irregular one, so he feels random scratches of sand and nicky rocks on his back and the backs of his legs. He starts rubbing himself.

¶ Todd lathers his dick in pH-balanced spit from his mouth. His mouth is a pond, full of algae. The ocean sounds like a highway. Todd's fist is a funnel, or a hot-dog bun, going up and down. Soon the tube releases its sputter of falling stars in the daytime.

¶ Then quiet. The sun grows hotter and bigger faster, a Beethoven symphony finally getting rolling. Todd stays indolent like a splayed starfish on this, his last beach day.

¶ Todd: (mumbling

out loud, but making

no sense, to a helicopter

flying overhead)

Drop a
bomb
on me.

It won't matter.

I'm a bone.

¶ Later in the

afternoon

he catches a

wooden ferry home.

—Brad Gooch, excerpt

from <u>Scary Kisses</u>

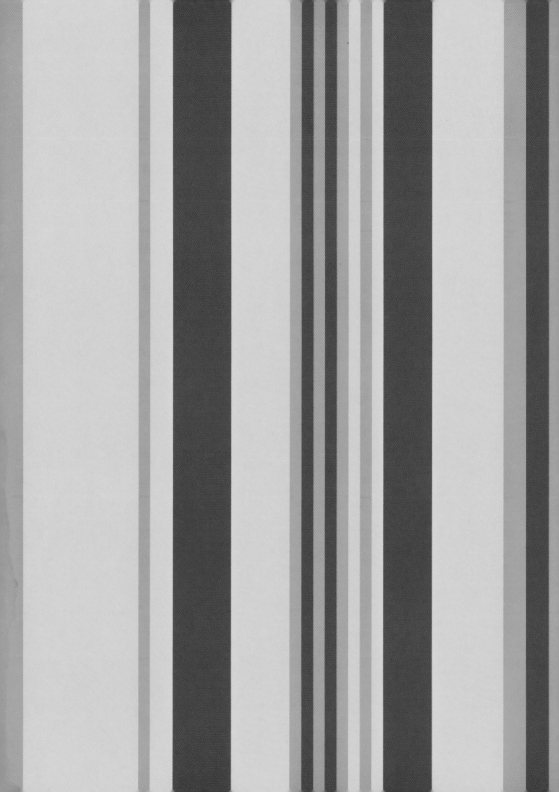

MEN IN THE MARSHES

3

DEVINE

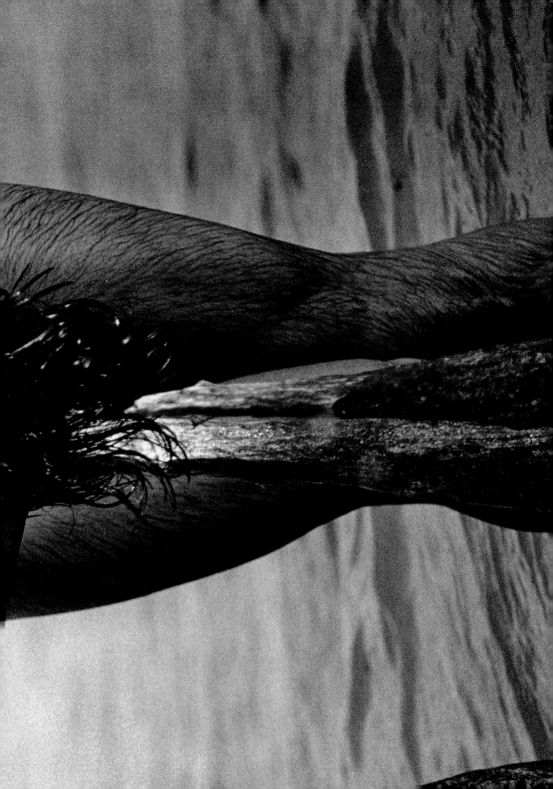

"Hardly had I anointed myself and experienced that first delicious stretching out in the sun (my head covered with Duncan's straw hat) when I heard a shout, gay and buoyant, coming from the

Sahara side of the wall. I sat up and saw a youth beckoning to me, greeting me, and then coming bounding like a puppy over the sands toward me. It was as though he knew me.

Skirting the seaward end of the wall he came around and was soon standing beneath me on the street side. He climbed up the slope of sand to just below my slab and smiled up at me.

¶ With that smile of his my heart leapt and my mind quickened to something inexplicable, uncanny—narcissistic if you like—but overwhelming: a flash of nostalgia, homage, recognition. This youth was me, my double: not as I was now but as I was some thirty years ago; or rather, what I would have been had I been truer to my destiny. He was, therefore, without flaw where I was marred; but the contours were the same, the attitude of body the same, the texture of the skin; the auric coloring, the shape of the face, even the spirit looking out of the light-blue eyes—all the same. This was no vague association or envious wish of vicarious juvenescence. It was the certainty of identity. I knew it in that glance: an identical style, his as naively fresh and innocent as mine once was, yet with that unexpected satyr twist to it, that half-faun, half-angel gaze, half heaven, half earth, which had kept me forever trying to find Christ in Apollo and the saints on Mount Olympus. I was humbled, I was stunned.

¶ He stood with his feet apart, wriggling his toes in the hot sand and looking up at me—speaking in Turkish. He wore a bathing slip and though I was still naked his eyes showed no surprise. I know no Turkish but I understood what he was saying, "Come and swim with me." "Yes, I will."

¶ I climbed down from the wall and together we ran toward the sea. "I could be running with my once young shadow," I thought. His bare feet flew over the sand so lightly they could have been winged. We sported in the waves for perhaps fifteen minutes, standing or treading water every now and then to communicate. Then, true to that insidious impulse that drives me to sever relationships, just as they are forming, I told him I had to go. I gestured toward my wall, inviting him there, but it was too late. The spell was broken. He radiated a Dionysiac smile, waved, and leapt away over the sands.

¶ I am as prepared to believe that none of this happened as that this was no mere human stripling who bounded into my ken on that magic afternoon among the ruins of a Greco-Roman town. Angel, double, god or satyr, to what purpose had he come? If he was Hermes, with what message for my future? Fool, fool, why did you dismiss him? My eyes scanned the shore. He had run into oblivion. I never saw him again." —Paul Roche, excerpt from With Duncan Grant in Turkey

MEN IN THE SHADOWS

SWEET

4

So what is it about
the sun that makes
one so brainless?
All I remember of
that week with lily
was the sun, the
cool June air, the
empty beaches
reaching away as

we faced the
glittering sea, the
sea grass blowing
in the dunes
behind us.

I
don't
remember
it
ever
being
night.
I
don't
remember
eating.

We must have, but what? And the food was from where? I remember none of these things.

¶These are the other fragments of that week on Fire Island I recall. I'm in the water naked. It's chilly. Our Illy with his big willy is hovering around at the edges of the blue, blue water. Dancing about like a three-year-old. Dipping in a toe and darting back.

His body looked like an Ingres drawing. All sloping lines, one honey-tan color, honey-blond hair standing straight up, slanting Oriental eyes.

¶A beach taxi was coming. Being naked on the beach wasn't that common then, so I gestured to him to come into the water. To not shock the solid burghers who might be in the taxi on their way to Ocean Park. Illy didn't understand. The crashing waves covered the sound of the taxi's motor. And then it was whizzing behind him. He whirled around, giving them a real flash. Surprised, he threw himself into the ocean, sinking that beautiful body from their sight. I laughed. It was high delight in those chilly, blue waves, sparkling in the high sun, the dunes behind, long grass blowing, the taxi churning away down the beach, sexy, tan Illy stroking his way through the water toward me.

—David Leddick, excerpt from The Sex Squad

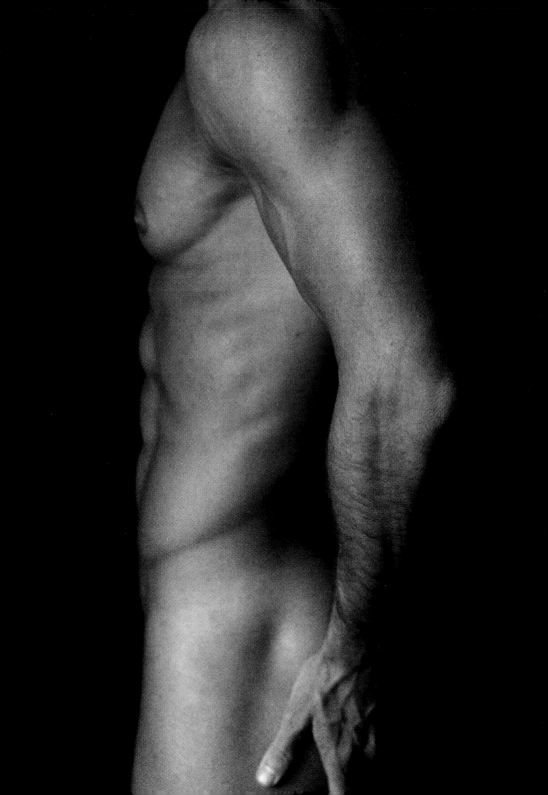

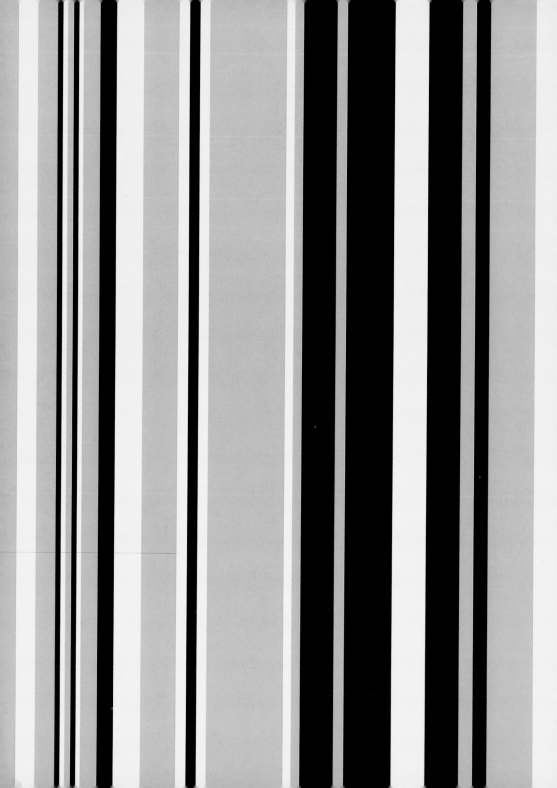

MEN ON THE SHORE

ALI 5

There were also the summers we spent at Fire Island Pines, three words of lament for Paradise Lost.

What it is these days I don't know;

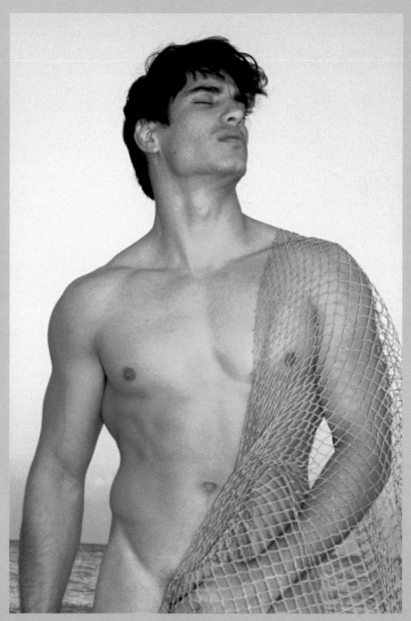

what it was then beggars description.

Each time the ferry left Long Island and headed for that enchanting sliver of scrub pine and windswept dunes, it felt like leaving the moorings of all the mores and social taboos I'd ever known. Once on the island, it was like living inside the most romantic of Technicolor movies: no cars, no traffic but tanned bodies in bathing suits no matter where, on the beach or in the stores or strolling the boardwalks on the way to another lunch or brunch or tea dance or trick or dinner or party. Every weekend a dozen parties. Was it the Black and White party, or the Red, White, and Blue party, or the Black and Blue party where the deck gave way under the weight of a hundred gyrating pumped and polished bodies and then after a moment's shocked pause everyone resumed dancing, but now on a tilt? Was it the South Seas party or the Aztec party or the Cleopatra party where Sam Sloman as Mae West made his entrance from the bay, borne in a litter by a half-a-dozen bodybuilders?

¶ A few years before when Paul and I had gone to the Pines, the parties had been elaborate, with queens spending weeks of time and salary on their costumes. I recall a Roman orgy party Paul and I attended with a couple of friends, me dressed as Tutankhamen attended by three Egyptian gods. Our pleated linen skirts were made at Hattie Carnegie's, our gold lamé crowns at Lily Daché's. By the time I knew Brian, however, the parties had become much more simple and relaxed. Someone was giving a poolside party with a Tahitian theme? You threw on a bathing suit, stuck a flower behind your ear and a joint in your basket, downed a tab of mescaline and you were out the door. Ahhh, all those brilliant colors in the sparkling sunlight, all those glistening bodies on parade, all those pink and turquoise drinks, all those pills and tabs and joints. I was high one afternoon lying on the beach (Brian was in LA), when out of the water came Cal Culver, soon to become America's first gay porn star as Casey Donovan in <u>Boys in the Sand</u>. It happened exactly like it does at the beginning of the movie: he walked up to me, I got up, and without saying a word we walked into the woods. I was still high later that day when I said my name to the clerk in the grocery store so I could charge the food. That's when the guy behind me said, "Did you ever write a poem called 'Vermeer'?" I had, and he'd read it in the Berkeley literary magazine; in fact, it was one of his favorite poems. What a nice feeling that was—but so unusual, for I'd grown unaccustomed to relating to people on any basis other than my looks.

¶ We talked outside the store and agreed to meet the next morning for breakfast to continue our conversation. Then I met a terrific kid on my way back to the house, and that made me late for drinks, after which I stopped by another trick's place to say we'd better move things back an hour, but one thing led to another until I was two hours late for dinner, which meant I lingered over coffee to compensate, and then some people insisted I stop by for another joint on my way back to the second trick's place before going to the Boatel, and that must have been where I passed out. I awoke the next day around noon, having forgotten my breakfast date with the guy who'd liked my poems, having forgotten I'd ever published poems or done much of anything I could take pride in besides being constantly desired and envied.

¶ That was one of the two summers a friend rented a room in his house to Brian and me for a hundred dollars. The friend knew dozens of beautiful young boymen, which meant that every weekend the house was glutted with beauties, so there were interminable waits for the bathroom and quarrels over who usurped it the most. I was actually fairly fast: a shave and a shower and a final primp, then the injection in the right cheek of my ass with one of the syringes Ben had prepared for me back in the city. Then off into a night of dancing at the Boatel on another of the highest highs I'd ever known. —Alan Helms, excerpt from Young Man from the Provinces

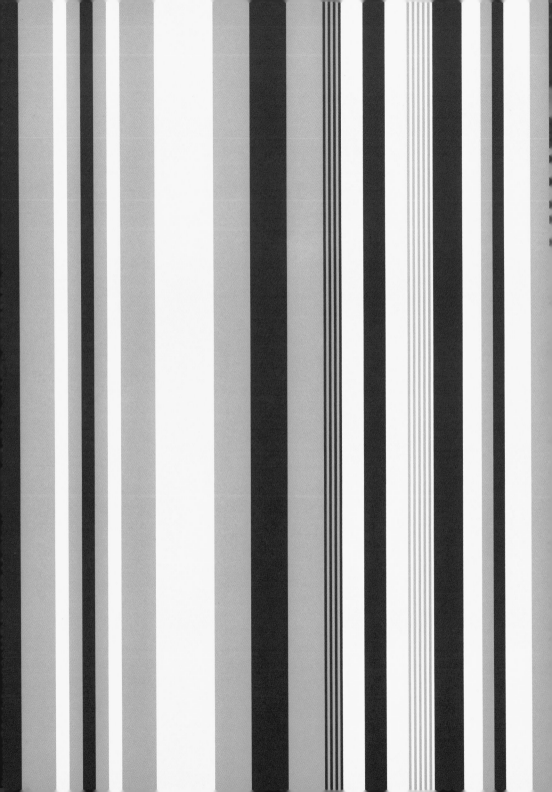

MEN ON THE BEACH

6

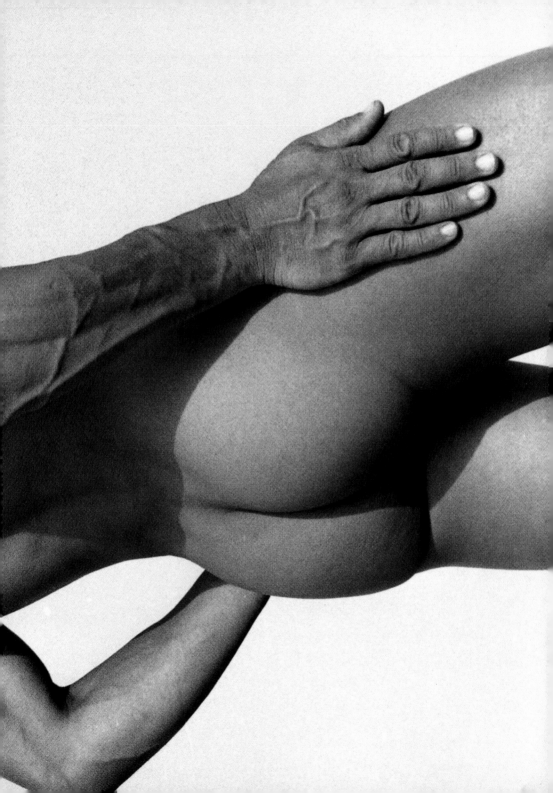

What was meant by Queer? That was maybe another trick
above my head, like "excellent, exquisite, excrement,"
which my father, Frank, and his good friend Victor rolled
out at each other and then hollered (nor could I tell about
the laughter, which often seemed like barking). Now they
were calling my favorite beach Queer's Beach, but it was
really Two Mile Hollow, the sign said so. I was thirteen

years old and needed to get in shape, needed to become
much better than I was, pledged to walk to the beach
every day, which round-trip took two hours. That includ-
ed the time walking more slowly on the sand from Two
Mile/Queer's to Amagansett and back. In winter, the sun-
set was electric blue and orange. The walk home then

was very dark and cold. It was always possible, especially since it was not a very nice sounding word, that
when they said "queer" they meant me, Elizabeth.
¶1975 - Awareness came like an unfortunate moss. No.
Should I not use the word "awareness"? "Now I knew, it
had crept upon me like . . ." Knowledge, awareness, the
eyes wide open. Beautiful queer young men were not the

corruption, especially those at the beach because unlike
unqueer beautiful young men, these said hello to me and
smiled. No, the unfortunate creeping stuff had much
more to do with the loud laughter and the jokes from the
yellow-teethed unqueer men, and the thin, depressed
women. In summer you had to go to the beach early,

before noon, and have the soft salty air wash over you while you lay in shorts and tee shirt on a freshly laundered towel. The beach was the one example of depth that was not frightening.

¶1981 - Now it is fall, and August's muggy air has been cleared finally, like a sozzled gentleman escorted from the American Hotel Bar. Walking to the beach is prefer-

able to bike riding because solitude has a slow pace. There has been a hurricane. The waves at Queer's Beach (still the best beach) are cutting across every direction, thundering into each other and only finally getting pushed sideways to the shore. The sand is flat, with a hard crust, and an armada's worth of wood is strewn everywhere. Yet the sky is now that deep, saturated blue that comes when autumn exhales the pressures of summer. The unqueer people from the seventies all seem to be out of the glamorous work that gave them license to scorn. I have been away, and look eagerly for the regular solitaries. But it is an odd time of day, and there has been this storm. Queer—that puzzling word.

A person who has to squeeze through some impossible definition. Now I'm one who says, "some of my best friends are . . ." Thank God for leaving home. But at the beach, the ocean so roiled, my poor heart is unconsoled, it wants to stay queer. —Maryellen Hannibal, excerpt from The Pornographer's Daughter

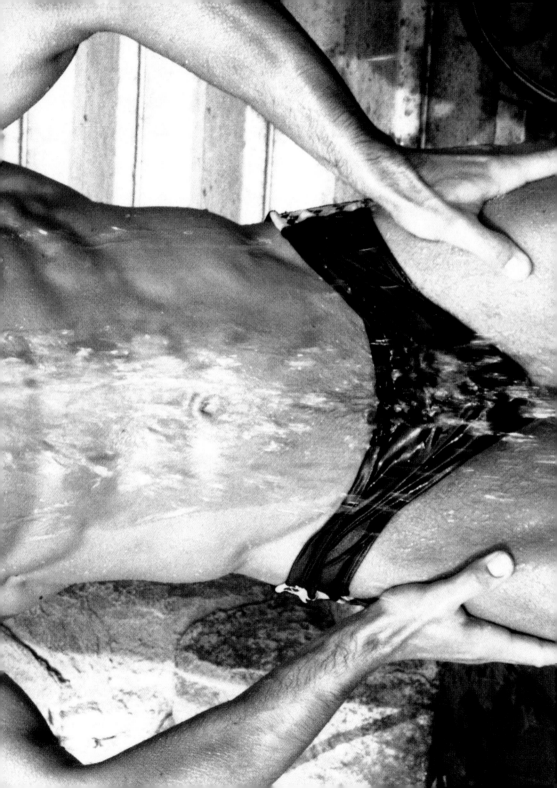

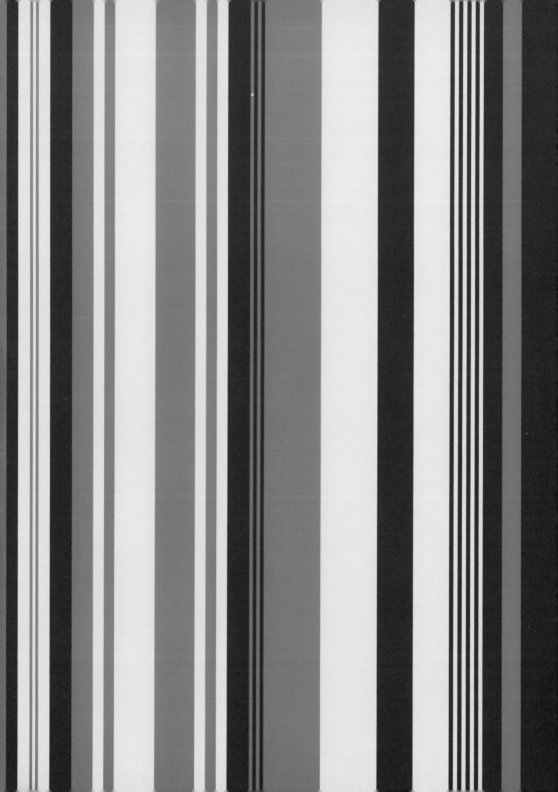

MEN IN THE WATER

7

RODRIGUEZ-DUARTE

By
the
sea,
by
the
sea,
by
the
beautiful
sea.
You
and
me,
you
and
me,
Oh,
how
happy
we'll
be.

When
the
waves
come
a'
rolling
in,

Then
we'll
float
and
fool
around
awhile,

Ma
is
rich,
Pa
is
rich,

We
will
sink
or
swim,

Over
and
under
and
come
up
for
air,

So
what
do
we
care?

I'd
like
to
be
beside
your
side
beside
the
sea,
beside
the
seaside,
by
the
beautiful
sea.
—Popular
song,
1914

I would like to thank:

Dianora Niccolini,
whose beautiful photographs
of men in the sun
first inspired this book.

Sandy Gilbert,
my first editor
at Universe,
who liked the idea and
nurtured the book.

Charles Miers,
Publisher
of Universe Publishing,
who always has lots of
enthusiasm and lots of guts.

Margaret Braver,
my good-tempered
and charming final editor,
who brought this book
into the light of day.

Jason Losser,
my art director,
who is so handsome
you are surprised
by all the creativity
and organization
he brings to a project.

And,
all the richly
diverse photographers
and studly models
whose many talents
made it possible
for this book
to find its place
in the sun.

Salvatore Baiano

Salvatore Baiano
Back Cover: Dianora Niccolini

Photographers:

Salvatore Baiano is a native of Italy who now works as a photographer in Miami Beach. He specializes in both female and male nudes.

Dianora Niccolini is perhaps the foremost woman photographer of the male nude. Her work has been seen in many exhibits and books. Born in Italy, she came to the United States as a child and now lives in New York City.

Andy Devine won prizes for his male nudes while still in school in California. Later his career took him to Miami Beach. His work appears in a 1999 calendar. He currently lives in Los Angeles.

Dick Sweet has been a ship captain for over forty years on all the seven seas. He has photographed the male nude all over the world. He now lives in Newport, Rhode Island.

Ali is a major Miami photographer. His work has appeared in many exhibitions and is published frequently. Born in Cuba, educated in the United States, he now lives in Miami Beach.

Patrick Sarfati is a famed French photographer. His work is seen in magazines, on CD covers, and in many exhibits. Born in Tunisia, educated in France, he now lives in Paris.

Alexis Rodriguez-Duarte was born in Cuba and spent his early years in Miami. Widely exhibited, his work has appeared in important fashion magazines and his portraits include many celebrities. He now lives with his partner, Tico Torres, in New York City.

Writers:

Quentin Crisp is a native of England and an icon in the United States. He is a writer, best known for his autobiography <u>The Naked Civil Servant</u>. He is ninety this year.

Brad Gooch is famous for his important biography of the poet Frank O'Hara. He is also a novelist and lives in New York City.

Paul Roche is a well-known poet and also a translator of the Greek classics. He was a favorite model for the English painter Duncan Grant. He lives on the island of Mallorca.

David Leddick is the author of novels and photographic books of the male nude. He lives in Miami Beach and Paris.

Alan Helms is a professor of English at the University of Massachusetts in Boston. He was acclaimed for his autobiography, <u>Young Man from the Provinces</u>.

Maryellen Hannibal is a novelist living in San Francisco with her husband and daughter. She also writes educational textbooks and is a TV panelist in her hometown.